CN00806500

10 special walks in La Alpujarra

7 full day walks and 3 half day walks

Patrick Elvin

LIST OF WALKS   **PAGE**

INTRODUCTION

These walks are inspired by a fabulous walking holiday I enjoyed in 2017 with a group of friends based in Atalbeitar, in a marvellous medieval house, which served as a perfect base to do these stunning walks .
http://www.albaholidaylets.com/casaaloe/house-village)

I have had previous experience of walking in La Alpujarra as I have also walked the entire GR 7 from Lanjaron through to the Puerto de la Ragua, and also the entire GR 142 from Laroles to Lanjaron. On other occasions I have walked up and down Mulhacen twice whilst combining other walks around Trevelez . And on a further occasion I had three days exploring the Poqueira valley .

These walks are the best of of all these experiences and I recommend the month of May as the best month in which to walk this area; the temperatures are still reasonable and the countryside is at its best .

THE BOOK AND HOW TO USE IT

The book is a no frills practical guide to walking in the central Alpujarra between Pampaneira and Trevelez . It contains for each walk , brief statistics and description, how to get there , usually two maps and a profile , and Lat and Long references at key points of the walk using decimal degrees from Google Earth .(to check go to TOOLS then options then 3D view then check the show lat and long box is ticked under decimal degrees)

The maps are pdf downloads from http://www.juntadeandalucia.es/institutodeestadisticaycart ografia/lineav2/web and are at scale 1:10000.   The numbers I have added along the routes drawn on the maps refer to key moments during the walk and appear in the text.

The other maps show distances in kilometres during the walk and come from www.mapometer.com or www.wikilocs.com and can all be found on those websites and uploaded to your device. The background is google earth . Just type in the title of the walk under search or use the weblink I have placed below the map .

SIGNAGE

In the past 20 years Spain at local and national level has introduced the European system of path marking . This consists of:

1:   red and white markers for long distance paths (Gran recorridos) (GR) examples found here are the GR 142 and the GR 7 the Tarifa to Athens path

2: yellow and white markers for medum distance paths (pequenos recorridos) (PR) generally linking villages together.   You will see these frequently on these walks .

3: green and white markers for local paths (senda local) (SL) .Created and marked up by town halls and are paths that start and finish in a particular village .

An extract from the guide to footpaths in Andaluica

GR-142
The GR-142 crosses the Alpujarras, but takes a lower route than the GR-7 or GR-240 Sulayr, meaning that it is generally less challenging.

Pequeños Recorridos (PR)
PRs are all possible to do in a day, ranging from a couple of hours to more challenging 7-8 hour walks. Many of our routes are PRs in their entirety or else coincide with them along certain sections. PRs are generally marked in yellow and white.

Local marked trails
There are quite a few marked local trails that don't have the status of a PR. These are often marked with white arrows.

Rights of way

A network of old droving routes or rights of way (known as *Vias Pecuarias* or *Cañadas Reales*) criss-crosses the Sierra Nevada and surrounding areas. These are often marked with green posts either side of the track (see far right). (these will not be found in these walks .)

MORE BOOKS ON WALKING

GUY HUNTER WATTS - Walking in Andalucia published by Cicerone

CHARLES DAVIS Walking in the ALpujarras

Patrick ELVIN Walks around Gaucin and Walks in the Serrania de RONDA published by Amazon

WALK 1 BUSQUISTAR – RUTA MEDIEVAL AND THE ESCARIHUELAS

Time: 5 hours
Difficulty: medium
Terrain: path , road, track then path

Brief description: A spectacular walk if you choose the tougher options but even if you dont you enjoy great views and interesting history . The road sections are quiet and never dull.

HOW TO GET THERE   Enter Busquistar from the Pitres to Trevelez road down Calle de Albaicin . 100 metres after a sharp right hand bend past a bar and before the church take Calle San Felipe down to the left . There is parking down here. Look out for a sign board on the left displaying information on the PR 299 Ruta Medieval .

START : start at the display board heading east : at the end of the road as it turns sharp right down the hilll take a track to the left indicated by yellow and white flashes known as the Camino del Molinillo

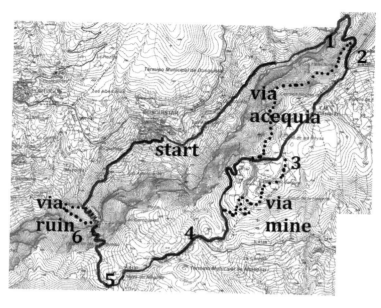

After 1 kilometre (15 minutes) take a right fork down the hill marked by Y/W flashes . Its a narrow path parallel to a track which it joins and then becomes a path down to the river Trevelez.

After following the river the path then crosses a bridge (MAP 1   36.947902° -3.272268°) and starts climbing the other side passing a ruin on the left 5 minutes after the bridge .   After 10 further minutes there is a welcome bench where you can catch your breath. A few metres further there is a gate the other side of which there is an interesting display board explaining the history of the Acequia (irrigation channel) . A classic example of which is a few metres further on. (MAP 2   36.947773°   -3.269054°)

You have a choice here depending on your fortitude and head for heights. If you are feeling brave follow the acequia on its right bank heading south for about 2 kilometres until it joins the road above (The wikilocs track follows this route) The author confesses the day he did this walk the rest of the group did not have the appetite for this excitement)

The alternative route entails continuing above the acequia on the PR 299 until you reach the road . Turn right and follow the road direction Almegijar A4130 . You can avoid part of the road section by cutting through the large quarry that appears on your left ignoring the prohibido signs . (MAP 3   36.935706° -3.278028°) Keep to the left hand side of the workings to pick up a track that after passing over the hill zigzags down rather laboriously to the road below . Turn left and follow the road until you reach a junction . (MAP 4   36.926840° -3.287923°)

Ignore the left turn A4128 and veer right keeping on the A4130 for a further kilometre as far as a track to the right leading up the hill to some houses known as the Cortijo de Panjuila . (MAP 5   36.922225° -3.297682°) After about 100 metres take the right hand fork marked by a wooden footpath sign heading down the hill.

After 5 minutes and passing a fertile vegetable smallholding on the left the track becomes a vertiginous path zigzagging down the steep side of the Trevelez gorge.
There is a great view point at the start of the escarihuela (zigzag path) where you can see the villages of the La Taha community laid out before you , (Mecina , Fondales , Ferreirola, Pitres, Atalbeitar, Portugos and Busquistar , not forgetting Capilerilla .

At the bottom you cross the river Trevelez by a ruined mill
(MAP 6   36.927904° -3.300720°   ) and you can either
take the steep zigzag path up the other side or the more
gentle path to the left passing a ruined farm before turning
right onto the GR 142 which will return you to Busquistar .
Keep right where there are options to ensure you arrive at
the bottom part of Busquistar and your starting point

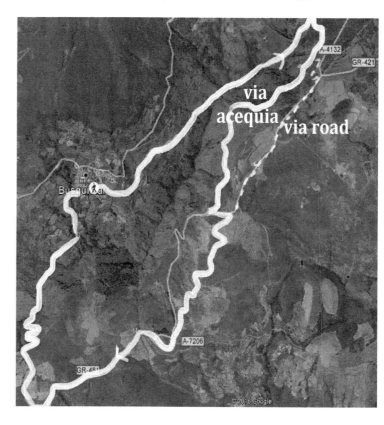

Wikilocs track goes via the acequia
https://www.wikiloc.com/wikiloc/view.do?id=1143502

WALK 2 - ATALBEITAR TO FERREIROLA CIRCULAR

Time: I hour (2.3 Kilometres)
Difficulty : easy
Terrain: small paths, some road

Brief description: A very short introduction to 2 of La Taha
´s villages . This should include a stroll around both villages
to enjoy the architecture and simple style of the villages

How to get there .

Take the road from Pitres to Portugos and turn right down
to Atalbeitar. Park in the car park at the entrance to the
village . (no cars allowed in the village)

START : Walk back along the road for a few metres and by a
pylon take a rough track off to the left . After a few metres
the track becomes a path and you follow it as it passes by a
couple of houses then continues down hill eventually
emerging onto a small tarmac road.   (MAP 1   36.932941°
-3.317254°)

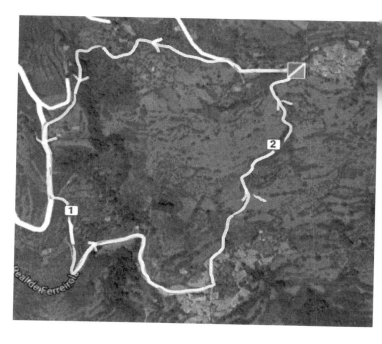

mapometer showing distances in kilometres

https://gb.mapometer.com/walking/route_4541605.html

Turn left and go almost 200 metres and look for a track to the left which splits in 2 directions ; one to a house to the left and to the right down a rough path leading down hill. (MAP 2   36.931389° -3.317001°)

Take this right hand path and follow it down hill until it emerges onto a track which soon becomes concreted and continues downhill to meet a tarmac road .   (MAP 3 36.929616° -3.316560°)

Turn left and after 5 minutes arrive in Ferreirola . Pass the church on your right and then take the opportunity for a stroll around the picturesque streets , noting a wash house on the left a few metres past the church , where you need to return to . (MAP 4   36.929731° -3.313339°)At the wash house turn left up a narrow street which is the PR 299 , ruta medieval to Atalbeitar . Follow this route which soons becomes a path all the way up the hill back to Atalbeitar .

When you arrive In Atalbeitar take a wander around this tiny village where there is an art gallery and an unofficial bar and cafe .

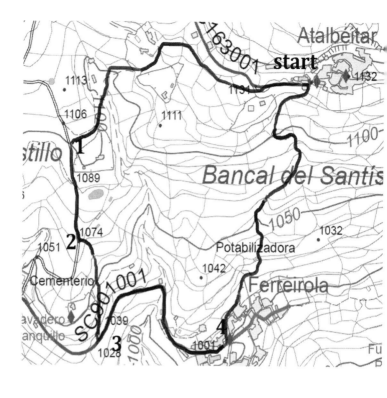

MAP FOR WALK 2

WALK 3 ATALBEITAR TO BUSQUISTAR VIA THE MEZQUITA

Time: 2.5 hours 6.5 kilometres
Difficulty : easy
Terrain: mainly footpaths , one stretch of road

Brief description: A walk with many interesting features including a sparkling water spring , a ruined mosque and a stroll through Busquistar and Atalbeitar .

HOW TO GET THERE From Pitres take the road to Portugos A4132 and take the first road to the right signposted Ferreirola and Atalbeitar . Then take the left fork to Atalbeitar and park at the entrance to the village .

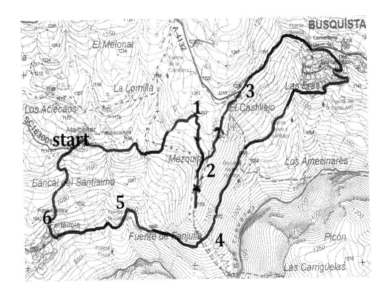

START :   walk through the village following the GR 7 and PR 299 signs signposted to Busquistar . You will be on a footpath which follows the contour line to start with and after passing close by a house turns up to the left passing entrances to exotic looking fincas in the trees . When the path emerges into more open country and levels out onto a plateau look for a green metal gate on the right . (MAP 1 36.935551° -3.302751°   ) It leads to a field and further down to a rocky ridge. At the end of the field look for a path leading firstly slightly to the left of the ridge and then crosses over to the right hand side . The path passes between rocks and bushes, a little indistinctly in places but the general aim is to follow the ridge down until you reach a collection of ruined houses one of which must have been the site of a small mosque , subsequently built over.

Retrace your steps and after 5 minutes look for a path off to the right of the ridge which will lead you up the slope to a rough track and then on up to the road. (MAP 2 36.934187° -3.301652°   ) (if you miss the path just return to the green metal gate and turn right to resume your route joining the main road after 5 minutes) .   (MAP 3 36.936739° -3.299827°   )

Turn right on to the road and continue until you reach Busquistar . Fork right down into the village on Calle Albacain and 100 metres after a haripin bend to the right there is a concrete road off down to the left called Calle san Felipe . After 200 metres Look out for a display board for the PR 299 . Drop further down the hill on the concrete road and head back just below the village looking for the GR 142 and PR 299 signs to get you heading south out of the village in the direction of Ferreirola . (Do not go left eastwards down the hill on the GR 142 direction Notaez/ Castaras) It starts off as a track, descends very steeply as it leaves the village and then joins another track coming down the hill from the right .

After this the route is on a path and you will pass a turn off to the left leading down to the valley floor and the Rio Trevelez . (MAP 4 36.930656° -3.301826°) You can make a detour (20 minutes) down this zigzag path to the ruined mill turning right just before the mill to return to the main route . Otherwise ignore this left turn . The path follows the contour line crossing two small streams on the way and then you will come to a spring with amazing sparkling water exiting from a pipe . (MAP 5 36.930746° -3.309071°)

Shortly you reach Ferreirola and you need to look out for a wash house on a right hand corner , just before the church . (MAP 6 36.929741° -3.313333°)

Turn right here and follow this concrete track then rough path back up to Atalbeitar (part of the PR 299 Ruta Medieval) . Turn left to return to your car .

mapometer showing distances in kilometres

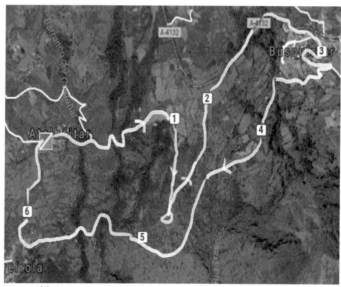

https://gb.mapometer.com/walking/route_4544095.ht
ml

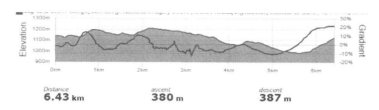

WALK 4 BUSQUISTAR TO MECINA FONDALES CIRCUIT VIA LA CORONA

Time: 5 hours (13 Kilometres)
Difficulty: medium
Terrain: paths and track , one stretch of road

Brief description: A walk which encircles the Rio Trevelez crossing it twice using the traditional path known as an escarahuela.   Great views up and down the rio Trevelez and to distant mountains.

HOW TO GET THERE   Enter Busquistar from the Pitres to Trevelez road down Calle de Albaicin . 100 metres after a sharp right hand bend past a bar and before the church take Calle San Felipe down to the left . There is parking down here. Look out for a sign board on the left displaying information on the PR 299 Ruta Medieval.

Distance
13.21 km

ascent
807 m

descent
805 m

Mapometer showing distances in kilometres

https://gb.mapometer.com/walking/route_4544303.ht
ml

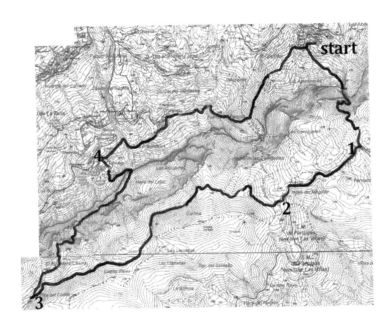

START   the walk at the display board for the PR 299 take the concrete road descending below you heading right and then take a left as it heads back up into the village .

This is the GR 142 direction Cadiar and Castaras, marked with red and white flashes. Follow this path down to the Rio Trevelez where there is a ruined mill and a bridge.   Climb up the other side on the zig zag path known as an escarahuela and emerge , 2 kilometres from the start, on to a road . (MAP 1 36.926924° -3.288015°) Turn right and follow for 1 kilometre where you will find a turn off to the right up a track leading to a couple of houses . (MAP 2 36.922155° -3.297793°)   Pass two houses and keep straight on ignoring one track down to the right. You will now stay on this track for about 4 kilometres skirting and then descending the hillside on your left with the Rio Trevelez on your right.   You pass through woods. As the track levels out there is a track off to the right almost doubling back on yourself.   (MAP 3 36.912187°   -3.330985°) This is the GR 142 coming from Orgiva heading to Mecina Fondales, with a misleading time on the waypost in your direction , showing a time at least an hour longer than you will take.

Follow this exciting track then path down the hill passing abandoned mine buildings and then zigagging down the rockface towards the river Trevelez . It heads north with Mecina Fondales on the opposite side . Cross a bridge and the path veers left up the slope and after 15 minutes arriving at the bottom end of Mecina Fondales . Head towards the north end of the village to find the continuation of the GR 142 direction Ferreirola . This is a delightful path passing through smallholdings before suddenly arriving at an alley in Ferreirola . Pass through this very attractive village and continue on the GR 142 towards Busquistar . 5 minutes further on there is a spring known locally as the Fuente Gaseosa , where the water comes out a little sparkling and is very refreshing to drink .

Continue, passing a turn up to the left and two further paths to the right and Busquistar will come into view . When the track divides, take the right fork which will take you into the lower part of Busquistar and it is then a matter of keeping along the bottom part of the village to rejoin the track you left the village on at the start of the walk . Or you can wander up into the main part of the village for refreshments .

WALK 5 - THE RIO TREVELEZ NORTH OF TREVELEZ

Distance: 12 Kilometres (4 hours)
Difficulty: Medium: some tricky navigation
Terrain: mainly rough footpaths , can be muddy along the river

Brief description: an attractive walk with not too much climbing , the first half above the river with great views and the return along the banks of the Trevelez.

HOW TO GET THERE   Take the A 4132 to Trevelez and park in the main square where the road passes through the lower part of town (Plaza Francisco Abellan) .

START the walk facing the upper village and take the street to the right of the fountain and then bear right up Calle Ladera . At a wash house with a virgin bear right . This street soon becomes a track running parallel to the Rio Trevelez below to your right and then gently descending to river level . When you arrive at the river turn right to cross over on a concrete bridge and head up this track to pass a farm on your left , At a signpost indicating two routes up the Peñabon take the left hand path (MAP 1 37.007480° -3.256857°)   soon passing a building on your left and then crossing over an acequia .

Shortly afterwards the waymarked route turns right up the hill . You continue straight on and from now on there will be no waymarking to assist you until you rejoin the river for your return leg . You need to be careful with your navigation until you reach the river.

MAPOMETER LINK SHOWING DISTANCES IN KILOMETRES

https://gb.mapometer.com/walking/route_4545791.html

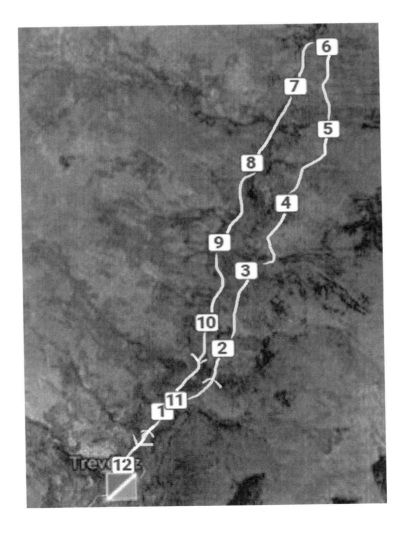

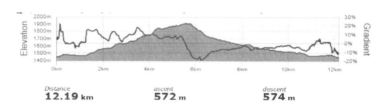

The path climbs gently then passes to the right of a ruined farmstead with a threshing floor . The path descends after this and crosses a gully. You pass another farm on your left , with solar panels on the roof. Continue climbing and where the path divides take the right fork climbing up towards a stone building .

The path crosses another gully, goes through a fence then follows an acequia before climbing once again. It then levels out, passes above a threshing floor and then climbs indistinctly towards a holly oak .

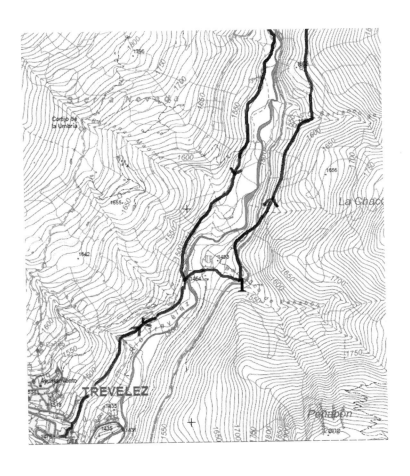

MAP OF FIRST PART OF WALK (AND RETURN)

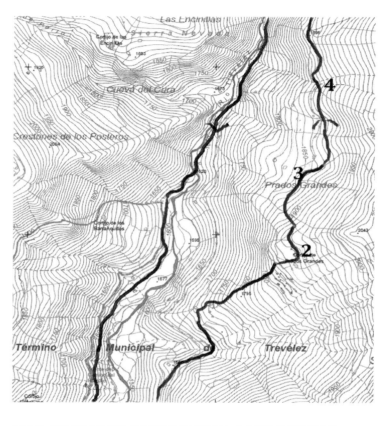

MAP OF SECOND PART OF WALK (AND RETURN)

The path then climbs up to a farmhouse . Pass to the left of the building and then up the side , ignoring a path heading down the hill. (MAP 2   37.026390° -3.242726°)At the top of the buidling turn 90 degrees to the left and walk along the contour line through scrubby bushes looking for a path which starts fairly level , passes a ruin on your left and then forks right (ignore the left fork going down hill) and up the slope towards some craggy rocky outcrops. Pass through a wire and post gate and enter more open country.

Leave a solitary farm to your left ,   (MAP 3 37.031456° -3.242730°) climb a little to pass another ruin a bit overgrown with bushes and then follow the contour line towards a fence . Pass through (the author was unable to find a gate) and look for two ruined buildings amongst the bushes and trees ahead . The right hand one is hard to see as it is overgrown with bushes and trees. Pass between the two buildings and follow a faint path up the stony slope the other side . When you come to a disused acequia follow this as best you can and soon a faint path heads down the hillside. (MAP 4   37.035852° -3.241214°) There is a path up to the right at this point which you ignore. .

Your next landmark is a farmhouse ahead (Cortijo de Chordi)and below you with a solar panel which you aim for passing through a wire and post gate and descending fairly rapidly to reach the threshing floor in front . (MAP 5 37.043203° -3.241822°) Pass in front of the house and turn left onto a path which will take you down to the river . (MAP 6   37.043529° -3.243419°)

MAP SHOWING TOP PART OF THE WALK

From here back to Trevelez is easy to follow. You first keep to the left hand bank of the river and after about 30 minutes you cross over the river on a bridge. From then on you remain on the right hand side of the river until you arrive at the bridge where you crossed over at the beginning of the walk . Stay on the right hand side of the river and take the same track back to the village of Trevelez that you started the walk

WALK 6 - TREVELEZ PEÑABON CIRCULAR

Time: 3 hours
Difficulty: medium
Terrain: track to start and finish otherwise rough paths

Brief description: an exciting walk rewarded after a steep climb with views towards Mulhacen and the Trevelez valley

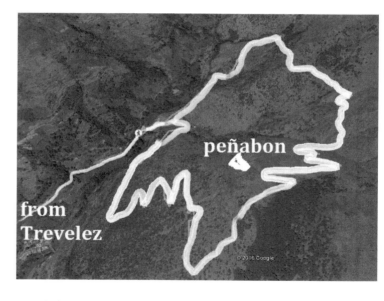

Track from wiklocs
https://www.wikiloc.com/wikiloc/view.do?
id=13039837

HOW TO GET THERE   Take the A 4132 to Trevelez and park in the main square where the road passes through the lower part of town (Plaza Francisco Abellan) .

START the walk facing the upper village and take the street to the right of the fountain and then bear right up Calle Ladera . At a wash house with a virgin bear right . This street soon becomes a track running parallel to the Rio Trevelez below to your right and then gently descending to river level . When you arrive at the river turn right to cross over on a concrete bridge and head up this track to pass a farm on your left , At a signpost indicating   the SL A 78 two routes up the Peñabon (MAP 1   37.007570° -3.256635°)take the left hand path soon passing a building on your left and then crossing over an acequia .

Shortly after the acequia there is a junction of paths. Take the right hand path up the hill which is waymarked. You will follow this path all the way to the top. It climbs first seemingly away from the Peñabon then turns south to cross precipitous barrancos at times the path almost disappearing under landslides. Signs warn you of the dangers of landslides on two occasions. The final climb zigzags up the barren slopes of the Peñabon to arrive at a plateau . To visit the summit head right to the end of the outcrop at 2015 metres to enjoy views across to Mulhacen and up the valley of the Rio Trevelez.

Retrace your steps to the path and turn right to cross over the plateau (MAP 2   37.000242° -3.249340°) and down the other side . This is a shorter route , easy to follow which will bring you zizagging down to an acequia which you follow for a while before arriving at a boulder strewn barranco which you cross to find the notice board and the path you came up on . (MAP 3   37.007570° -3.256635°) Return past the farm , crossing the river and turning left to return to Trevelez.

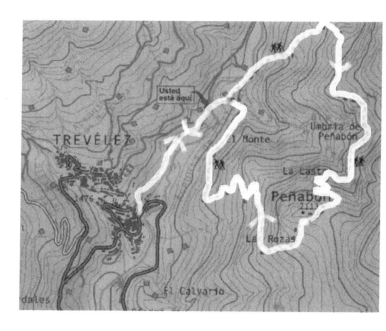

Map from the display board at the start of the ascent

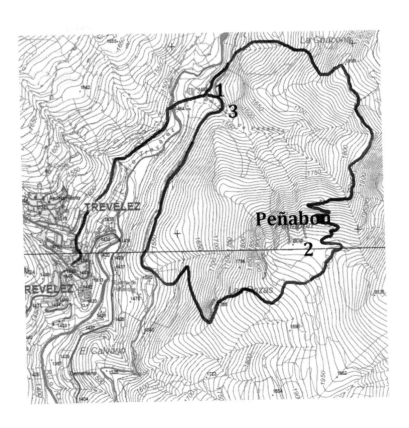

relief map of the walk

WALK 7 THE POQUEIRA VILLAGES CIRCULAR

Time: 6 hours 18 Kilometres
Difficulty: medium
Terrain: First part mainly small paths, the return leg has a track and paths and passes through three villages

Brief description: A very varied walk passsing through terraced fincas , crossing the Poqueira on four occasions , returning via an abandoned village and an acequia and passing through three thriving villages .

HOW TO GET THERE   Drive to Pampaneira . From Orgiva direction take the first car park on the left as you come up the hill . From Pitres enter the last car park on the right as you come down the hill. Park here

Start at the car park below the entrance to Pampaneira.
Facing up the valley take the narrow street in the middle of
the side of the car park in front of you. You quickly pass
through this lower part of the village dropping down to a
track which descends to arrive at a bend in the road.   For
the first part of the walk you follow el sendero Pueblos del
Poqueira (PR- A -70) for 5´5 Kilometres leaving it a short
time after crossing the The Chiscal bridge and although
there is virtually no sign posting , the path is well
maintained.   There is a panel displaying Sendero Local La
Atalaya . Follow for 2 K which is also the PR 70 . Pass
Barranco del Cerezo where there is a simple fountain with
iron laden water . The path descends towards the rio
Poquera.   Pass the ruins of Molino Placido Bajo and cross
the river on Puente de Pampaneira near area recreativo La
Poza. (MAP 1   36.946994°   -3.362856°)

Take a right fork climb to the west doing zigzags Pass
alongside la Acequia Cachariche, climbing between walls .
Arrive at Cortijo Haza Polvo where the first climb finishes
and continue on PR 70. (MAP 2   36.944368°   -3.367500°)
You descend below the cortijo through a meadow and
head north and arrive at the Barranco de los Herrerillos;
descend the Barranco, ariving at a post marking the
junction of the path to Bubion crossing by puente del
Molino. Ignore this right turn and continue north towards
Capilleira. (MAP 3   36.957344°   -3.365164°)

You start another ascent passing by ruins of cortijos
highlighted by Cortijo de los Majales and above this cortijo
the Era de los Majales.   You continue the gentle ascent until
you come to the Barranco de las Rosas o de los Pradillos.

You eventually arrive at Barranco de Haza Redonda, where you start the descent joining with the Sendero Sulayr (GR 240 (MAP 4   36.966965° -3.364891°) just before reaching the Puente Chiscal o Chiscar which crosses the Río Poqueira over a deep gorge and starts the climb towards Capileira . After 5 minutes you reach a small gully where you turn left off the main path (MAP 5   36.967269° -3.361900°) on to a small path which heads towards a ruined cortijo and shortly joins up with the PR A 69 Sendero de La Cebadilla. Turn left here to follow for a few kilometres.

This path drops down again to the rio Poqueira. Arrive at Puente Abuchite, cross over and climb again;, pass by an era, climb more north passing more ruins to reach Cortijo Abuchite, beyond which the path meets a track from which you can see las Casas de la Cebadilla below the Central Eléctrica del Poqueira.   Turn right to descend once again to the rio and join a main track at the bridge. (MAP 6   36.989650° -3.350877°) 200 metres further upstream you will find the hydro station .

Return to the bridge, cross the river and follow the main track to the old village of La Cebadilla, heading south for 1.5 kilometres (20- 25 minutes), climbing gently, crossing the Barranco de la Cabañuela, Then come to the Acequia de los Lugares, where there is a PR signpost.   (MAP 7   36.976995° -3.355122°) Turn right   to follow the acequia for 1 kilometre. Just past a round water tank on the left, fork right, continue for

250 metres then fork right again to make a descent on a stony path called Camino de la Sierra which brings you to Capileira.

Walk down the main street and when you see a car park below on the right, head down through the car park taking a street at the end on the left which descends steeply leaving a wooded park on the left .

 At the bottom turn left onto a path (MAP 8 36.960277° -3.359508°) which will take you to Bubion reaching the main road just above the village . Head down through the streets to the church leaving it on your right , You will join the GR 7 which heads to Pampaneira leaving Bubion on the Barrio Bajo passing by the Fuente Hondera, (MAP 9   36.947829° -3.356849°)

The path descends steeply southwards crossing the Barranco del Cerezo with Pampaneira visible below After passing the old wash house and the Fuente Cerrillo arrive at the main square, then pass the church to reach the carpark where you left the car.

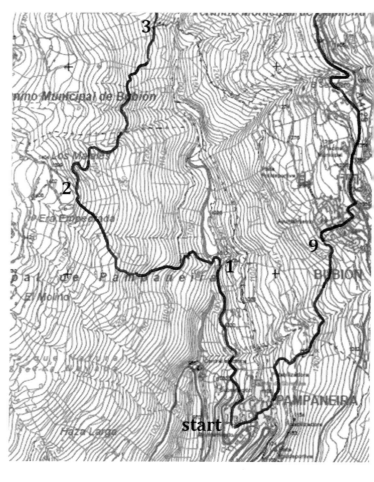

MAP 1 LOWER PART OF WALK

Wikiloc map showing route

https://www.wikiloc.com/wikiloc/view.do?id=11398876

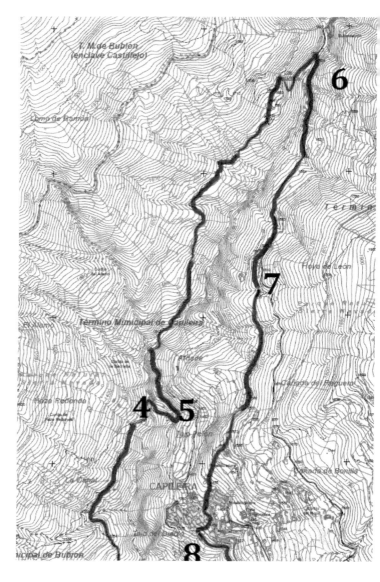

MAP showing upper part of walk

WALK 8 PITRES TO PORTUGOS CIRCULAR VIA CAPILERILLA

Time: 4 hours
Difficulty: medium
Terrrain. Tracks and paths

Brief description: A walk taking in three villages of La Taha , climbing fairly gently to 1740 metres . A more open walk than the gorges of the Poqueira and Trevelez .

HOW TO GET THERE : drive to Pitres and park in the main square having entered the village by the Calle el Puerto.

START: Facing the town hall.   head left and take the first street to the right (Calle La Virgen) After passing the farmacia on the right the road turns sharp left: Follow for 500 metres, where there is a turn off to the right which you ignore and 100 metres later take a track off to the left . 10 minutes later join a road from the left where there is a helipad down to the left. You bear right up the hill, the road bears sharp right passing a small circular reservoir, then does a zigzag before meeting the GR7 coming from Bubion. (MAP 1 36.938502° -3.346453°)

Turn right here to join the GR 7 and continue until it arrives in Capilerilla . As you pass the first two or three houses turn left into the main street (Calle Real de Capilerilla). As you leave the village you pass first the Ermita of San Francisco, then the Fuente de Pocillas.

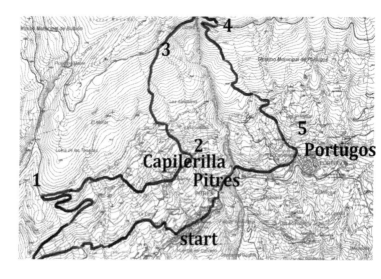

As the road does a loop to the right you take the PR A 29 to the left (MAP 2 36.944048° -3.323390°) which will lead to the Area recreativa de Portugos . The path climbs the hill running parallel to the Rio Bermejo on your right. Eventually you reach a track and here you turn right . (MAP 3   36.953459° -3.329977°) You cross the bridge called Junta de los Rios before arrving at the Area Recreativa the highest point of the walk with great views down across the Trevelez valley .

You soon turn right (MAP 4   36.954899°
-3.322541°) to follow the PR A 29 down the hill to
Portugos, crossing over a track on the way . Enter
Portugos on the Calle Eras and take the first street on
the right (Calle Churriana) which passes a wash house
by the same name. (MAP 5   36.942467°
-3.311975°)   After passing a calvary (Fuente de
Calvario) you cross the rio Bermejo as you join the
road (A 4132) to turn right to return to Pitres.

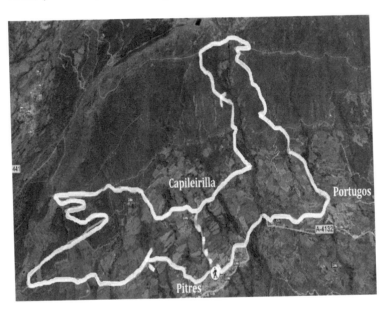

Map from wikilocs route

www.wikiloc.com/wikiloc/view.do?id=15512873

WALK 9 - UPPER POQUEIRA TO CORTIJO LAS TOMAS AND RETURN VIA ACEQUIA ALTA

Time: 6 hours   (17 Kilometres)
Difficulty: medium
Terrain: Maily rough paths , track to finish

Brief description: a dramatic walk climbing to over 2000 metres and returning the opposite side of the valley at one stage following an ancient acequia .

HOW TO GET THERE Drive to Capileira , pass through the village and on a right hand bend near the top of the village, park in the car park off to the left .

THE WALK starts in the top right hand corner of the car park . Take the path PR A 69 which climbs the hill out of Capileira. It meets an acequia . (MAP 1   36.968363° -3.356180°) Walk alongside the Acequia de Los Lugares irrigation channel below a replanted pine grove before moving uphill, crossing the irrigation channel and coming out on the track (MAP 2   36.974336° -3.356318°) which takes you down towards La Cebadilla the abandoned village supporting the power station. Cross the Rio Poqueira then pass by the Hydro Electric station built in 1950 then look for a sign board indicating the PR A 23 on the left , (MAP 3 36.992460° -3.349390°)   a path which zigzags steeply up the rocky slope .

After just under half an hour of continuous zigzagging you reach a fork; the path to the left follows the Loma Púa ridge towards El Veleta, but you take the gentler right hand route. A few minutes later pass another path leading away to the left next to a fenced in farmhouse, and come out onto a flat area overlooking much of the route lying ahead. In the distance, directly below the Mulhacén and the Refugio Poqueira shelter you can see the Cortijo de las Tomas, to which you will later climb. (From the top of the zigzags you will pass one farm house to your right, one ruin to your left then a farmhouse to the right with a threshing floor, then a farm to your left before dropping down to the river bed)

At the river (Naute) follow the riverbed, crossing the bridge over the river and arriving at the Cortijo de la Isla, a farmhouse which, to judge from its corrals and the threshing area further up, has not been flooded for many years despite standing in the centre of the watercourse. Further upstream you pass beneath Los Tajos de Cañavete and cross the river by a bridge located in an area of large reeds where there are the ruins of a farmhouse surrounded by cherry trees. The path climbs the slope out of the valley bottom and comes to another junction, where you take the right path leading down to the river. Pass through a muddy area half way up the slope and a few minutes later you come to the River Veleta, which you cross via a bridge.

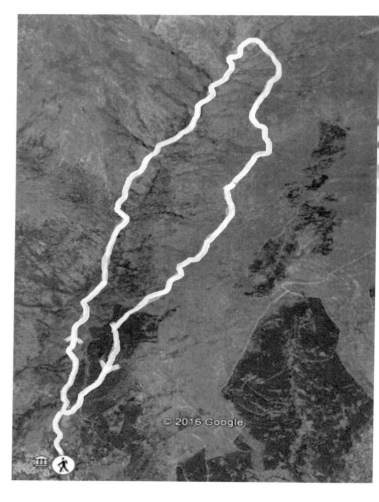

wikilocs map showing route with link below

https://www.wikiloc.com/wikiloc/view.do?
id=11398876

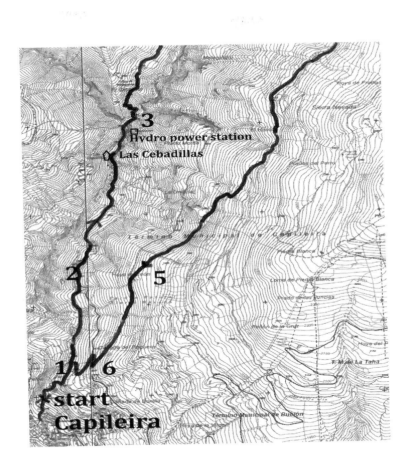

MAP 1 Lower part of the walk

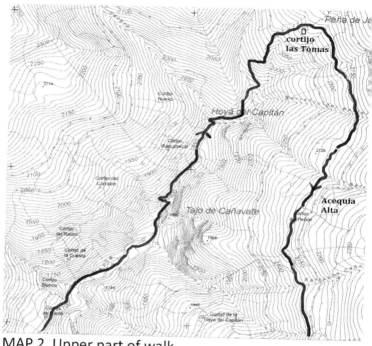

MAP 2 Upper part of walk .

Climbing further we come to the River Mulhacén (Rio Seco on Google Earth) , which we also cross before undertaking the strenuous north-easterly climb to the Acequía Baja. A little higher, we finally reach the Cortijo de la Tomas (2,100 m.). (MAP 4   37.017803° -3.330272°) The name Cortijo de las Tomas stems from the presence nearby of the two tomas, or water outlets, supplying the Acequias Alta y Baja, the two irrigation channels of Moorish origin which carry water to the La Taha area.

From the Cortijo you head back   towards Capileira southwards along a path which is at first flat but then climbs toward the Acequía Alta. This walk of approximately one hour between the two acequías (Baja and Alta) offers spectacular views of the surrounding area, including the magnificent headwaters of the Poqueira, an impressive natural amphitheatre which runs in a circle from the Pico Tajo de los Machos to Mulhacén at an altitude of over three thousand metres. The relief of the upper reaches of the Rivers Toril, Veleta, Río Seco and Mulhacén is clearly glacial.
.

You now come to Los Corrales de Pitres, below the Acequía Alta. This is an area still used for livestock breeding, a traditional activity in the Sierra Nevada where the abundant water, the gently sloping ridges and the climate have favoured the use of its meadows for grazing since the very earliest human settlements in the area.

Further on the path begins to descend. Cross the Acequía Baja and enter a pine forest via a firebreak corridor. Then turn left to join a driveable track coming from the right. (MAP 5   36.975900° -3.350094°)A few minutes later you come to the La Cebadilla track, which you cross over (right then left) to continue your descent down another track ahead. After a couple of tight curves you reach   the drinking water tanks and the acequia , where you turn left to rejoin the path leading back to Capileira along which you came at the start of the walk.

WALK 10 ROUTES UP AND DOWN MULHACEN

Time: from 5 to 9 hours
Difficulty: medium to hard
Terrain : track and rough paths

Brief description: this chapter is an attempt to explain the various possible routes up the Mulhacen . This is the holy grail of walking in the Alpujarra. Mulhacén is the highest mountain in mainland Spain (3479m or 3482m depending on which map you are using!). It is not a "technical" mountain in good summer conditions. There are paths ascending the mountain from three sides: south, east and west that allow Mulhacén to be climbed in a day. From the north it is not really possible to climb Mulhacén without a night out wild camping. The north face is the domain of climbers and scramblers. The routes described below are non technical ways up the mountain for walkers.

ROUTES

1 By BUS from Capileira

  The village of Capileira (1400m) has a National Park Information Centre and from here it is possible to book a bus in summer months up to Mirador Trevelez (2700m) where a lot of people start their ascent of Mulhacén's South Ridge. It is possible to reach the summit this way in 2 hours from leaving the bus. (5 K each way) It is important to book the bus in advance. This can be done either by calling into the information centre or by telephoning them. Details of the information centre and how to book are on the Sierra Nevada Guides website.

From the bus drop off take the first path to the right off the main track ahead marked with many cairns and follow all the way to the top ignoring any side paths , and return the same way. It is 5 kilometres each way with a height gain of 780 metres . (2700 to 3480 metres)

FROM HOYA DEL PORTILLO .

This involves drving up from the top end of Capileira about 13 Kilometres, up a forestry road that becomes a gravel track . There is a car park just before a barrier across the road at 2150 metres , the route is about 26 kilometres return (8 – 9 hours) .

Opposite the car park there is path heading up into the woods, after 20 minutes you emerge onto a fire break which you walk up to join the track which has done a loop to the right. The track immediately does a hairpin to the right where there is a mirador caled Puerto Molino. On the left there is a small path which you can follow for a more interesting route or continue on the track . These two

54

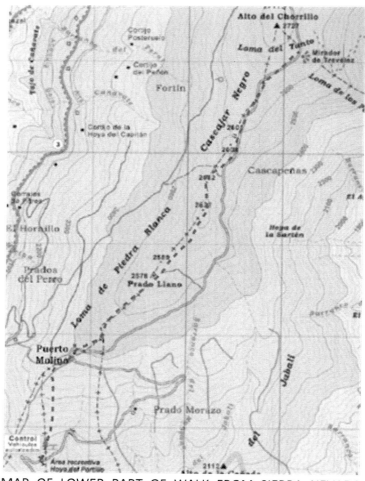

MAP OF LOWER PART OF WALK FROM SIERRA NEVADA
GUIDES WEB SITE

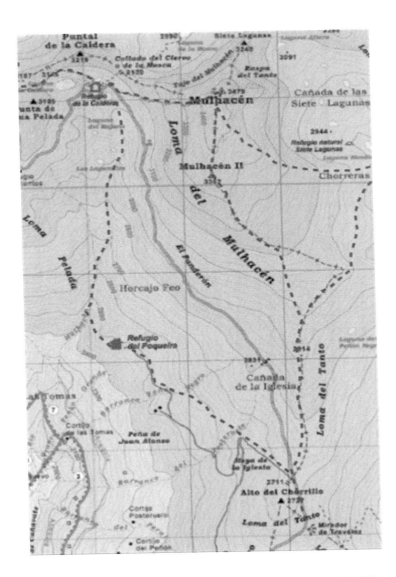

MAP OF UPPER PART OF ROUTE FROM THE BUS DROP OFF

routes rejoin after 30 minutes. You continue on the track
for further 30 minutes when you arrive at a junction of
tracks , left to the refugio Poqueira, straight on is the main
track and to the right is your path to the summit . Stay on
this path well marked with frequent cairns for the next 5
kilometres to reach the summit passing the false summit of
Mulhacen 2 on the way . The summit has a well decorated
shrine and a ruined building just to the right leaving you in
no doubt you have reached the top .

Either retrace your steps or for an alternative route go 50
metres back from the top and take a steep path to the right
down to the col below where you cross a track , pass by the
refugio de Caldera before taking the path down the slope
due south passing by the refugio Poqueira .

Follow the track towards the Alto del Chorillo and 2
kilometres after leaving the refugio on a left hand bend
take a path off to the right which is the PR leading back to
the Hoya del Portillo . It is well marked with yellow and
white and you only have to make one left fork after 3.5
kilometres where the path enters woods to climb slightly,
and then emerging onto the wide firebreak . There is a
marker post here and you turn right to follow the path you
started on back to the car park .

wikilocs track for circular route starting at Hoya del Portillo

https://www.wikiloc.com/wikiloc/view.do?id=2083944

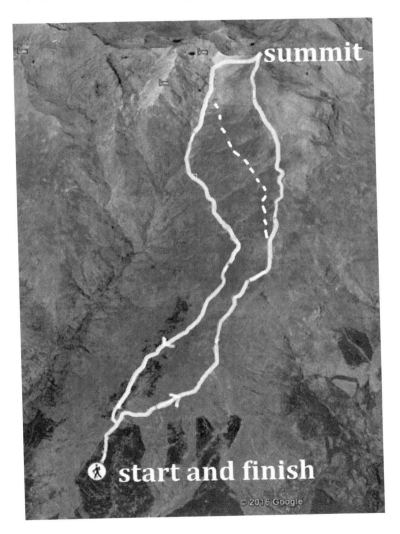

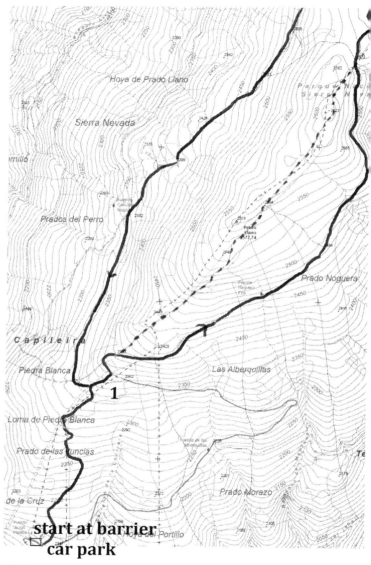

MAP 1 Lower Part of walk from Hoya del Portillo

MAP 2 CONTINUATION OF LOWER PART OF WALK

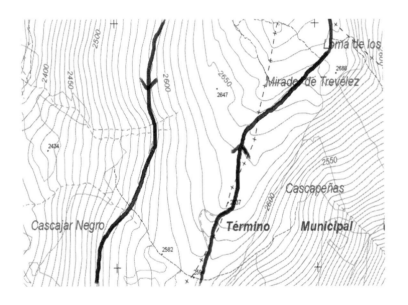

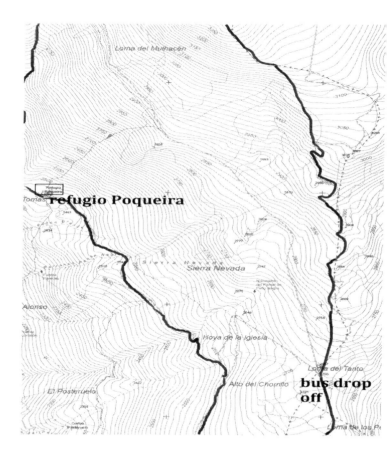

MAP 3 showing bus drop off point and refugio Poqueira

MAP 4 showing summit and start of alternative route back

FROM REFUGIO POQUEIRA

By using walk 9 to get you to the refugio Poqueira , (just continue past the Cortijo las Tomas to reach the refugio) and then take either route shown on MAP 3/4. The easier of the two options is to head to Alto del Chorillo and the bus drop off point and take the gentle path up which is very well marked with frequent cairns .   From the refugio it is 8 kilometres each way with a height gain of 900 metres.

http://refugiopoqueira.com is the website where you can reserve a bed and a meal

FROM TREVELEZ . There are two routes from Trevelez , one via the Mirador de Trevelez and the Alto del Chorillo and the other via Siete Lagunas .

I have done this way as a circular route   ascending via Mirador De Trevelez and descending via Siete Lagunas taking 9 hours in mid October on both occasions . The route is 23 Kilometres long and has a height gain of 1960 metres

This is the link to the wikilocs route as decribed above

https://www.wikiloc.com/wikiloc/view.do?id=17631880

This wikilocs route does the route in reverse

https://www.wikiloc.com/wikiloc/view.do?id=4984956

GLOSSARY

acequia   irrigation channel

arroyo   stream

ayuntamiento town hall

barranco gully

camino way

cortijo farmhouse

escarihuela   ancient zigzag path

farmacia chemist

finca smallholding

gran recorrido (GR)   long distance footpath

pequeño recorrido (PR) short distance footpath

rio   river

senda / sendero   footpath

Printed in Great Britain
by Amazon